AF413796

Your Valentine

This book is dedicated to my wife, Jordan.

— Anthony DeStefano

Note from the Author:

This children's book is based on ancient stories of a Christian bishop or priest named Valentine, who lived in Rome during the third century. Though details vary, its central elements — the secret marriages he performed, his imprisonment, his friendship with a jailer's family, and even the miraculous event involving the jailer's daughter — have all been handed down through Christian tradition for centuries. Though I have used imagination to supply dialogue and description, the main events you will read here are drawn from those time-honored traditions. Valentine has been venerated as a saint from the fourth or fifth century, and his feast day was officially established by the Church in the Middle Ages. He is remembered as the patron saint of love, marriage, and young people.

SOPHIA
INSTITUTE PRESS

Text Copyright © 2025 Anthony DeStefano
Cover and interior art Copyright © 2025 Antonio Javier Caparo
Endpapers adapted from: Heart confetti (410616454)
© annetdebar/ stock.adobe.com

Printed in the United States of America.

Sophia Institute Press
Box 5284, Manchester, NH 03108
1-800-888-9344

www.SophiaInstitute.com
Sophia Institute Press is a registered trademark of Sophia Institute.

print ISBN: 979-8-88911-556-4
eBook ISBN: 979-8-88911-557-1

Library of Congress Control Number: application in progress

First printing, 2025

Your Valentine

Anthony DeStefano

Illustrated by ANTONIO JAVIER CAPARO

SOPHIA INSTITUTE PRESS
Manchester, NH

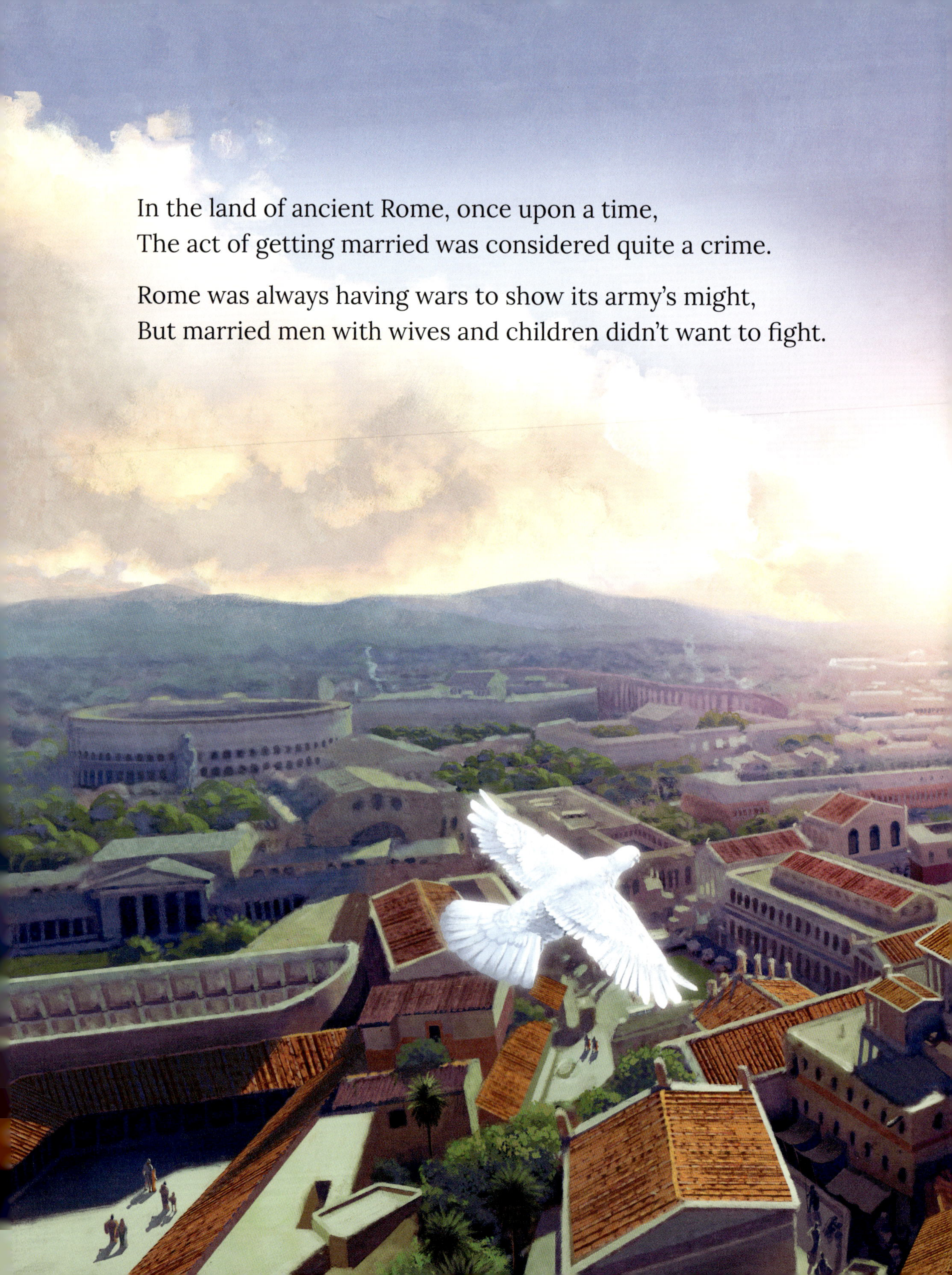
In the land of ancient Rome, once upon a time,
The act of getting married was considered quite a crime.

Rome was always having wars to show its army's might,
But married men with wives and children didn't want to fight.

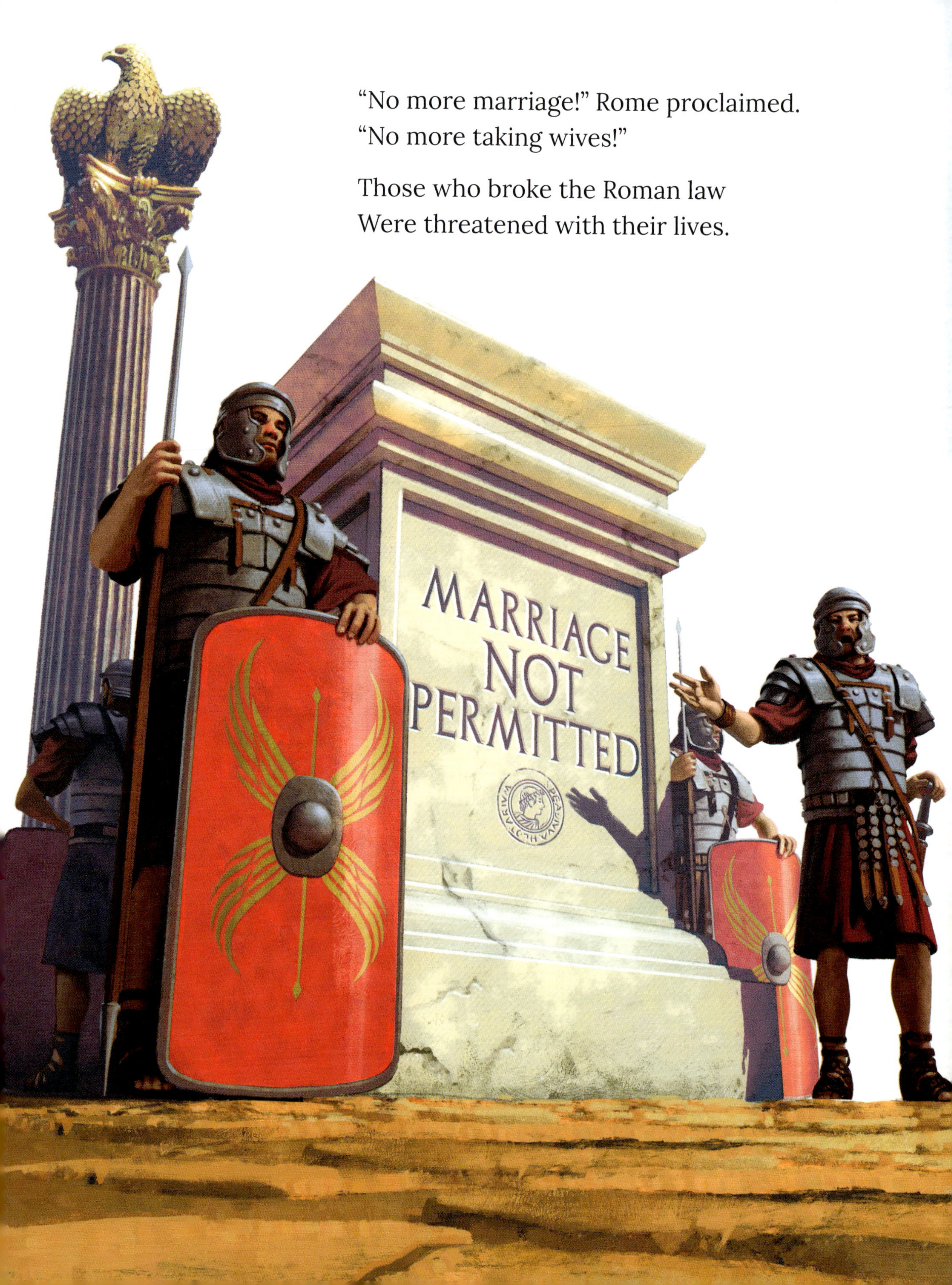

"No more marriage!" Rome proclaimed.
"No more taking wives!"

Those who broke the Roman law
Were threatened with their lives.

MARRIAGE NOT PERMITTED

But at that time, there lived a Christian, loving, brave, and kind.
He was a bishop of the Church whose name was Valentine.

When Christian couples fell in love and wanted to be wed,
Valentine would marry them in secret, it was said.

He told the couples whom he married they must never part,
Then gave them each a little gift — a cutout paper heart.

One day, soldiers caught the bishop with a groom and bride.
They took him to a prison, and they locked him up inside.

In the prison worked a boy; Marcus was his name.
He couldn't walk without a limp — his leg was weak and lame.

The jailer often yelled at him because he moved so slow,
But Valentine assured the boy: "It's not your fault, I know."

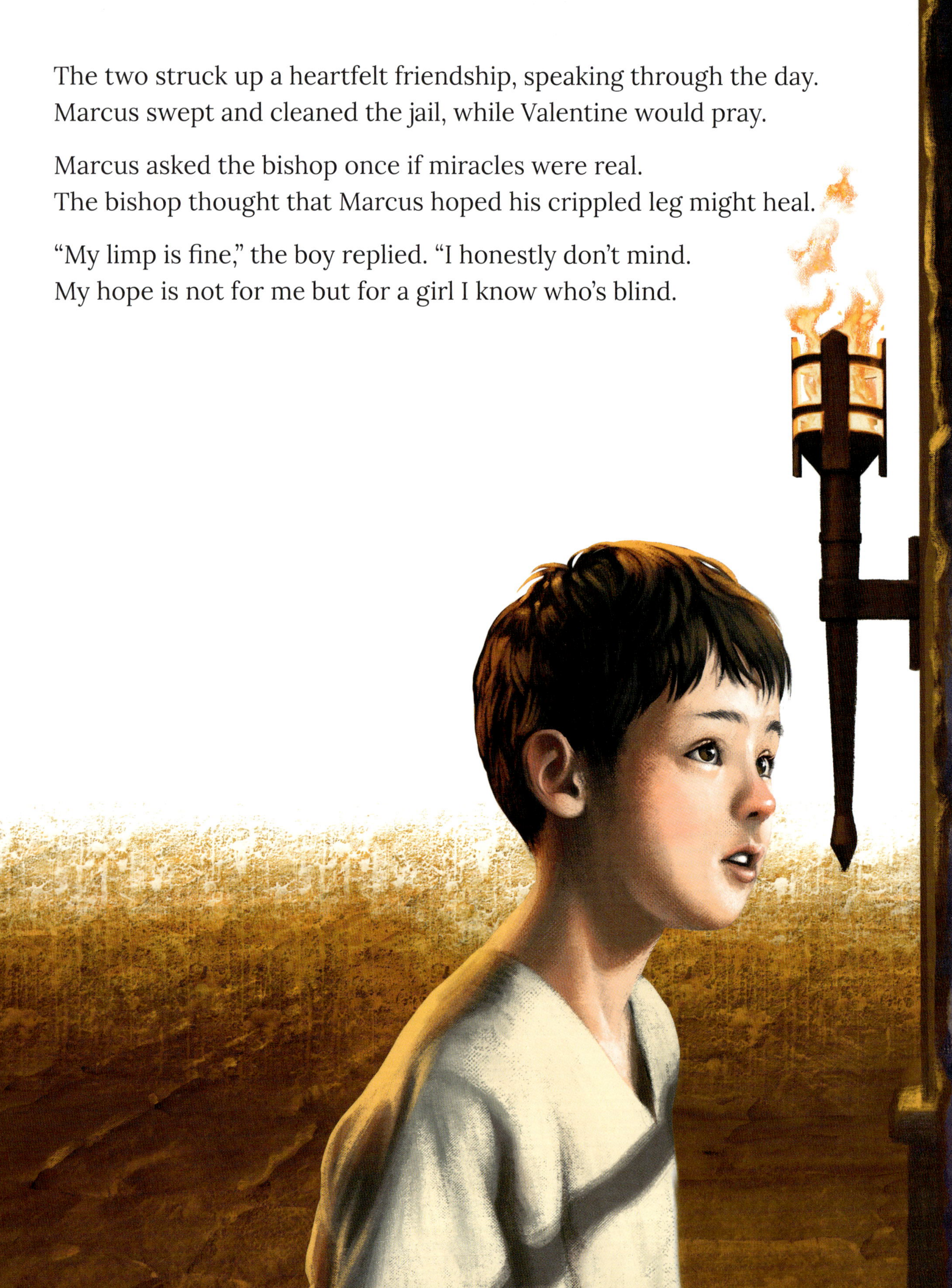

The two struck up a heartfelt friendship, speaking through the day.
Marcus swept and cleaned the jail, while Valentine would pray.

Marcus asked the bishop once if miracles were real.
The bishop thought that Marcus hoped his crippled leg might heal.

"My limp is fine," the boy replied. "I honestly don't mind.
My hope is not for me but for a girl I know who's blind.

"Marcella is the blind girl's name; she's kind and sweet and good.
I wish the God you talk about would help her if He could.

Her father is the jailer here—the one who's always mad.
He's really not a bad man, though; her blindness makes him sad.

All the children pick on her because she lost her sight.
They trip her, and they make her fall. It's mean and just not right!"

The bishop looked at him with love and smiled tenderly.
"With God all things are possible, so bring your friend to me."

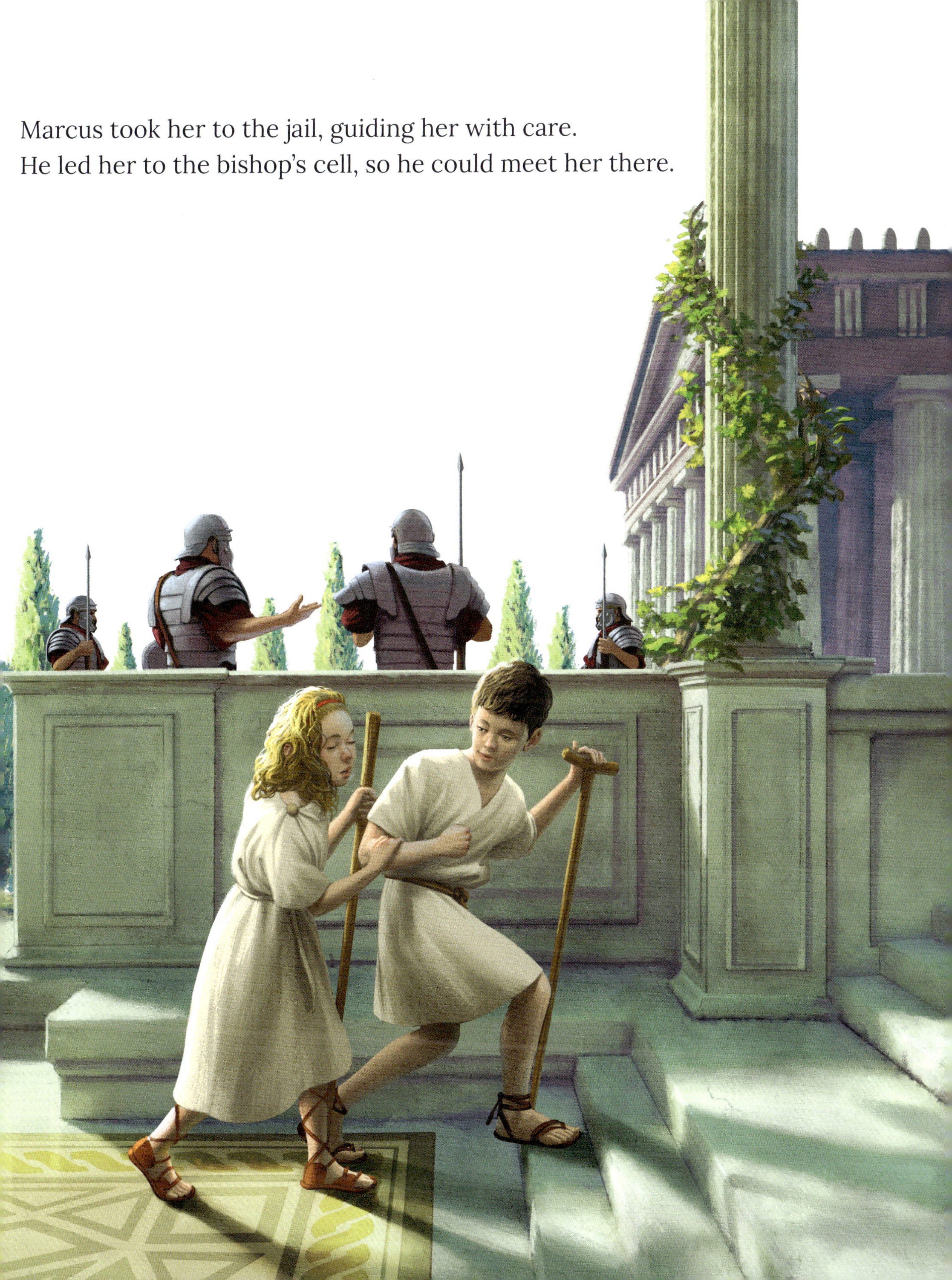
Marcus took her to the jail, guiding her with care.
He led her to the bishop's cell, so he could meet her there.

The bishop asked about her life and why she couldn't see.
She said she had an eye disease when she was only three.

She said that Marcus helped her walk and that he was her friend.
She said he was the only one on whom she could depend.

Marcella said her father couldn't see that he was kind.
The bishop said a person could have sight and still be blind.

The bishop took Marcella's hand; the blind girl felt his touch.
He said to her: "Dear little girl, God loves you oh so much!"

Just then the jailer thundered in and slapped the young boy's face.
"How dare you bring my daughter to this dark and dirty place!"

He grabbed Marcella's hand and left, shouting all the while:
"A prison's not a proper place to take a little child!"

After this the jailer kept his daughter far away.
But Valentine kept praying for her every single day.

Soon the Roman ruler came to visit Valentine.
He said, "You must give up your Faith to be a friend of mine."

"Never make a Christian couple into man and wife.
If you disobey this law, you must give up your life."

Valentine began to speak; the sun shone from above.
"Marriage is a gift from God. I'll gladly die for LOVE!

Love between a man and woman is a holy thing.
Joining them together can't be stopped by any king.

I follow only Jesus Christ!" the Christian bishop roared.
"Jesus is my Savior and my Sovereign and my Lord!"

The emperor, now filled with rage, looked him in the eye.
"There's nothing else that I can do! I sentence you to die!"

When Marcus heard about the news, he ran to tell his friend.
Marcella asked if he could take her to the jail again.

Despite his fear of being hit, Marcus said, "All right."
When the jailer went to sleep, he snuck her in at night.

The wind outside was whipping 'round and howling in the trees.
Valentine was in his cell, praying on his knees.

Marcella whispered through the bars, "They say you have to die.
People seem to hate you Christians. Can you tell me why?"

"The truth is sometimes hard to face," the Christian bishop sighed.
"Many people choose instead to hate it out of pride."

Then he smiled lovingly, and to her great surprise,
He reached out through the iron bars and touched Marcella's eyes.

He said: "Marcella, God is great. He loves and cares for you.
Do you believe with all your heart that what I say is true?

Do you believe that Jesus Christ can make your eyes like new?"
Marcella clasped her hands in prayer and bravely said, "I do."

The bishop prayed to God the Father, Son and Spirit too.
Marcella opened up her eyes, which now were sparkling blue!

She rubbed her eyes, then turned her head, and then she blinked again.
And for the first time in her life, Marcella saw her friend.

Suddenly the prison door came flying open wide.
The jailer screamed and cursed at Marcus, rushing from outside.

"You brought Marcella here again, you miserable disgrace!"
He took the crutch that Marcus used and waved it at his face.

Marcella quickly stepped between and told her father: "No!"
Her eyes were full of light and love; her face was all aglow.

Her father froze and shook his head in wonder and surprise.
He stopped his awful screaming, and he gazed into her eyes.

Then he dropped the crutch he held and fell down on his knee.
He hugged his little girl and cried, "My daughter, you can see!"

The jailer turned to Marcus and embraced the little boy.
He said, "I'm so, so sorry," as his eyes streamed tears of joy.

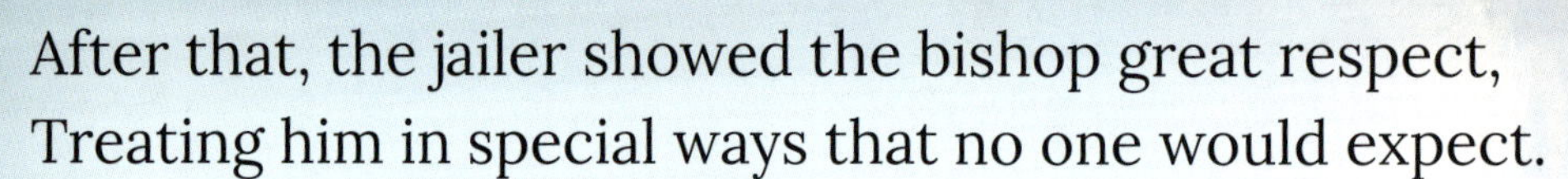

After that, the jailer showed the bishop great respect,
Treating him in special ways that no one would expect.

He felt so deeply grateful that his daughter now could see;
He asked if they could all convert to Christianity.

But soon the time approached for Valentine to meet his fate.
The fourteenth day of February was chosen as the date.

The night before the bishop died, he scribbled down a note.
He left it for the jailer's daughter; here is what he wrote:

"Dear little one, you precious girl, I'm happy you can see.
I'm going home to be with God, so please don't cry for me.

Remember God's great love for you; remember that, my friend!
And love that comes from God in Heaven doesn't ever end.

I pray the light that you've received will always brightly shine!"
The bishop signed the note *"with love"*
and closed: *"Your Valentine."*

When sunrise came and everyone was sleeping in their beds,
The Romans carried out their plans—and Valentine was dead.

They buried him not far from Rome, beneath a roadside cave.
Marcella placed a paper heart and roses on his grave.

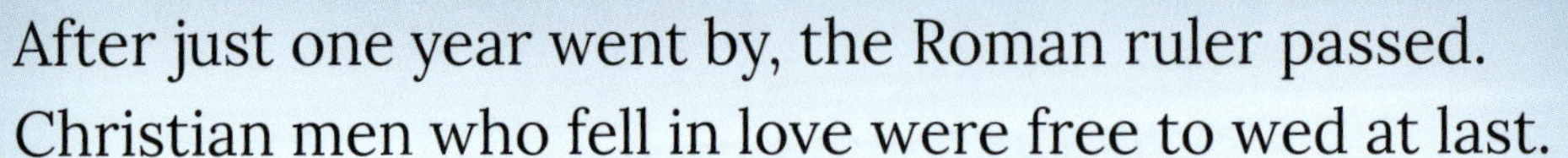

After just one year went by, the Roman ruler passed.
Christian men who fell in love were free to wed at last.

The boy and girl became adults and fell in love one day.
Marcus needed help to walk; Marcella led the way.

They married soon and spent their lives together side by side,
And tried to spread the story of the bishop far and wide.

Valentine became well known. The Church increased his fame,
Declaring him a holy saint, immortalized his name.

Today, we send out cards and hearts to those we hold most dear,
To honor this great saint whose light still shines so bright and clear.

For Valentine now lives in Heaven, watching from above.
He'll always be remembered as the saint who died for love.